The 7 Fruits of Budgeting

How to Create an Effective Spending and Savings Plan

ROSLYN LASH

THE 7 FRUITS OF BUDGETING, Copyright © 2018

This publication is designed to provide accurate and authoritative information regarding the subject matter covered. It is published and sold with the understanding that the publisher and author are not engaged in rendering accounting, legal, and other professional services. If legal advice or other professional advice, including financial, is required, the services of a competent professional should be sought. The author and publisher specifically disclaim any responsibility for any liability, loss, or risk that is incurred as a result, directly or indirectly, through the use or application of any contents of this publication.

All rights reserved. No portion of this book may be reproduced or transmitted in any form or by any means - electronic, mechanical, photocopy, recording, scanning, or others - without prior written permission.

The websites and references provided are considered correct at the time of publication. Changes after publication may impact the accuracy of the information.

Unless otherwise noted, scripture quotations are from the New International Version (NIV) of the Bible.

For information visit: http://www.RoslynLash.com

First Edition: April 2018

Contents

Contents i
Dedication iii
About the Title iiv
Introduction vi
My Story viii
Purpose of This Book xii
Budgeting Your Commitment 14
    I do not have time 16
    There is not enough money 16
    It is too restrictive 17
    I will spend it anyway 17
    My budget in the early years 19
    How to begin 22
    Asking why? 25
Kindness: Reducing Stress 28
    Needs versus wants 28
    Living beneath your means 33
    Keeping up with the Joneses 34
    Analyzing your spending habits 36
    Developing a workable spending plan 38
Goodness: Get Organized 42
    Setting goals 43
Discipline: Pay Yourself First 48
    Savings strategies for paying yourself 50

Methods of budgeting	53
Envelope system	53
Zero-based budget	53
Budgeting tools	54
Combination of budgeting styles	54
DYOB: Doing your own budget	59

Patience: Credit Cards and Impulsive Spending 67

My first lesson about credit	67
Advantages and disadvantages of credit	69
The cost of credit	71
The benefits of having good credit	73

Love: Money and Relationships 76

Whole love but divided bills	80

Faithfulness: Your Credit Score Matters 82

Joy: The Pleasure of Reducing Debt 87

Debt elimination options	90
Definition of success	93
Sacrificing	95
Moving forward	95

Reflections	101
Acknowledgments	103
About the Author	103
Appendix	105
Regular Budget	107
Variable Budget:	114

Dedication

I dedicate this book to my mother, Eunice Suber. There is not enough money in the universe to pay for the outstanding job that you performed as my mother. Words are too inadequate to express my love and appreciation for your unwavering love and guidance. Therefore, I am forced only to utter three simple words... I love you.

About the Title

The 7 Fruits of Budgeting focuses on seven of the biblical attributes known as the "Fruit of the Spirit." This biblical phrase (Galatians 5:22) addresses the attributes a person must possess to live a Spiritually fulfilled and Holy life.

Why did I choose only seven attributes? The number seven represents completion. It is also considered a lucky number. It gained its reputation from various references in the Bible. There are seven continents, seven days in a week, seven colors in a rainbow, and a host of other significant meanings for this Godly number. Therefore, I chose seven to demonstrate how using seven of the attributes will help you to create a complete and successful spending plan that will allow you to live a more financially fulfilled life. The attributes (also called "Fruits") addressed in this book are Kindness, Goodness, Discipline, Patience, Love, Faithfulness and Joy. Let me explain the significance of each fruit:

Kindness: Kindness, along with clarity, leads to insightfulness. If you are kind to yourself, you will avoid financial situations that lead to stress and discord.

Goodness: The fruit of goodness identifies the benefits of budgeting and the best strategies for creating an effective spending plan.

Discipline: Discipline requires that you exercise self-control in your spending habits. It allows you to explore your buying motives and prompts you to ask yourself the important questions such as, Can I afford it?

Patience: Patience is truly a virtue. It is imperative that you exercise patience as you walk through your financial journey. Practicing patience will prevent impulse buying. The less impulsive your actions, the lower your credit card balances.

Love: Love and discernment are necessary for you to accept your financial reality, and it will support you in making appropriate decisions. If you are in denial about your financial situation, your feelings are based on fear. Fear is the opposite of love. True love requires truthfulness. Therefore, you must be in full acceptance of your economic status.

Faithfulness: This term refers to being faithful to your word and being responsible for your actions. You must honor your commitments. A faithful person will commit to paying their bills on time, and if necessary, work through a debt reduction plan.

Joy: Joy is the feeling that you get when you have accomplished a goal. If you are stressed out about your bills, practicing the above Fruits will provide a joyous reward. You will receive joy from eliminating your debts.

Introduction

I would like to first congratulate you for reading this book. Your decision to seek knowledge and to financially empower yourself is commendable. You have decided not to learn about your finances haphazardly, and you have no plans to gamble on your future. You are making an intentional decision to learn how to manage your day-to-day money and how to increase your wealth. How can you become financially fit when you barely have enough to pay your bills? Believe me; there are ways to streamline your budget and remove "the fat," so to speak. You must be willing to make small sacrifices. (Remember, *sacrifice* is not an ugly word. Jesus made the ultimate sacrifice for us.) It is your money, your budget, and your decisions. Minor adjustments in your spending habits could yield great benefits.

For example, if you are spending $2.65 on a latte before work each day (assuming you work five days a week), that is $13.25 weekly ($2.65 x 5). You are spending $53.00 per month ($13.25 x 4) or $689.00 per year ($13.25 x 52) on coffee! You could easily brew your own coffee before going to work and save a nice chunk of change. This is just one small adjustment. Imagine if you made two or three changes in your spending habits.

Are you beginning to see the benefits of budgeting?

Maybe you already know the benefits but just don't see the need for writing it down. You think that you can keep track of it without going through the task of documenting what you spend. After all, you work 40 hours a week... you are smart enough to punch that clock (or computer). But let's be honest, being smart has little to do with money management. Your education and your salary have nothing, notta, nuttin to do with it. Your education has nothing to do with budgeting, just like using a GPS (Global Positioning System) has nothing to do with your driving skills. You need a GPS to direct you. A budget is similar because it directs your money. If you do not write down your budget (you can use paper and pen, a spreadsheet or an app), you will get lost just as if you were driving to your destination without directions.

Before I started documenting my spending, I would *lose* money. Initially, I thought that the bank teller miscounted and had short-changed me. Next, I thought that I might have dropped it. I would hope that the finder needed it more than me... 'cause I really needed it. After much thought, I remembered that I'd gotten gas ($25), picked up clothes from the drycleaners ($19), and bought a piece of cake ($6). That's $50! I realized that it was time to keep track of my coins. I started using a written budget and became a currency chaser. Have you had a similar experience? If so, you need a budget too.

Those that don't understand its benefits frown upon budgeting. In the following chapters, we will explore misconceptions. I'll share stories with you about my family, friends, colleagues, and clients. All names have been changed, and some details have been altered to protect the guilty... those guilty of money mismanagement. Of the guilty parties, my name is the only real name used. Believe me, I was so guilty!

My Story

My first full-time job after receiving my degree in Business Administration was in a Call Center for a major airline. At first, I loved the job, but around the tenth year, I began visiting bookstores daily to escape my mundane work life. That was when I was officially introduced to the field of *personal finance* – the management of money and financial decisions for a person or family. I constantly read books on personal finance and real estate. I read so many books that a friend told me that I needed to get my real estate license. After taking her advice, I resigned from the airline and accepted a position to utilize my homeownership and budgeting knowledge. That was my first official role in personal finance. However, I was unofficially groomed my entire life to make responsible money choices.

My mother is a survivor of the Great Depression of 1929. Growing up and into my adult life, I regularly heard stories of poverty, homelessness, hunger, and high unemployment. She shared stories that taught three morals: never live beyond your means, prepare for the future, and do not overspend. These stories translated into budgeting, saving, and minimizing debt. She would say, "You need emergency savings to prepare for life's challenges." The importance of being financially responsible was stressed. Although she encouraged me to strike a balance between saving and enjoying life -- she'd ask hypothetical questions such as, "What are you going to do if you lose your job, your salary is cut, or your car breaks down? Things may be good for you right now, but you're not guaranteed to have that job always." And as she predicted, life happened. I lost my job.

As a single parent, I was frustrated and scared. However, to some degree, I had followed my mother's teachings. I had maintained my credit, minimized my debts and made some decent investments. In retrospect, I wish I had made even more responsible decisions. I could have enjoyed myself just as much without excessive spending. I stopped using some of the items that I bought; so, I donated, sold, and threw away much of it. If I had spent my money more wisely, I would have had a nice savings account. Oh well, you live, and you learn. Fortunately, I didn't experience a major hardship after losing a salary of nearly $50,000.

Perhaps you are earning a higher salary and you think that $50,000 is minimal. What if you suddenly had a $50,000 reduction in pay? How long could *you* survive before experiencing repossession, eviction or foreclosure?

I can honestly say that since losing my job, I have not had a moment of insurmountable hardship. In fact, my family and friends noticed my seemingly stress-free lifestyle. My cousin once said, "I can't believe that you lost your job over two years ago and you haven't filed for bankruptcy."

Though appearances show something different, my life since losing my job has not been stress-free. If we compared my stress and bills with cream or milk, I'd say I am at the reduced fat stage. Let's look at heavy whipping cream. It is very thick, and you can use it to make something like quiche. If heavy whipping cream was a bill, we would be talking about rent/mortgage, car payment, credit card bills, student loans, childcare, credit card bills (Oops, I said that already). There's also whole milk. It is quite thick but not as think as whipping cream. If your finances are in the whole milk category, you are not being whipped but you are under duress juggling the bills. Then, there is reduced fat milk. It has a lighter weight. If you are in the reduced fat financial category, you aren't worrying about bill collectors calling. Congratulations, but you still must strategically plan because one major slip up could be disastrous.

Lastly, there is the fat-free milk category. This is the ultimate financial goal. This is where you can do what you want when you want without consequences or worry. For those that are approaching this category, a BIG CONGRATULATIONS!

Anyway, considering that I have worked as an Entrepreneur since losing my job, my journey has been amazing. I am not telling you this to brag because I cannot take the credit for my survival. I give *all* the glory to God. I will only toot my horn (toot, toot) for having the wisdom to listen. I stayed in prayer and followed God's directions, and I listened to the life lessons that my mother shared. And believe me, she shared a lot!

I still have a tough time wrapping my brain around how I survived my job loss. I didn't merely survive. I thrived while earning my Accredited Financial Counselor (AFC®) certification. I enjoyed myself by going to the movies, to dinner, to an occasional concert, and I even managed to take a few vacations including a cruise to Jamaica (Hey Mon!). I lived on a fraction of what I previously earned. What is even more amazing is that when my car was totaled in an accident, I bought another car. How? I can't explain it. Oh sure, I can tell you the steps of how to buy a car (and I wrote an article entitled "Tips for Buying a Car" which was published by *NASDAQ* and other media outlets). However, I cannot explain how I could afford it on my new meager income. It's impossible to describe. I have no words. It's incomprehensible. It's a God thing! The only way that I can comprehend it is by equating my survival to a story in the Bible:

> *Taking the five loaves and the two fish and looking up to heaven, he gave thanks and broke the loaves. Then he gave them to the disciples, and the disciples gave them to the people. They all ate and were satisfied, and the disciples picked up twelve basketfuls of broken pieces that were left over. The number of those who ate was about five thousand men, besides women and children.* ~ Matthew 14: 18-21

At first glance of this passage, you would think that 5000 people were fed. This is not the case. Scripture states that 5000 *men* were fed. This figure excludes the women and children. Therefore, if each man was married with just one child, there were easily 15,000 in attendance. Jesus fed the multitudes! And yet, there was food left over. Understanding this mind-blowing concept has helped me to understand how I survived ---by His grace!

Purpose of This Book

Everybody wants more money (well, maybe not Jeff Bezos or Bill Gates), and many people need more money. But let's keep it real, most of us could live comfortably on what we already earn if we simply managed better.

Mastering money management skills is more than just balancing your checkbook, and it has nothing to do with your intellect. There is a direct correlation between your spending habits and the way you manage money. If you want to take control of your money, you must first take control of yourself. If you expect to read this book without modifying your behaviors, you are wasting your time. There is no magical solution. It requires work. However, it is not hard work. The steps I will outline are practical and easy to implement. They require an open mind, diligence and commitment. If you are unwilling to follow the suggestions or lack dedication, this book is not for you. However, if you are ready to reshape your future and want to live more comfortably, continue reading.

Managing money has more to do with your habits and your mindset than it does your GPA or your IQ. Therefore, before we look at what steps to take and how to budget, we will determine if there is an underlying reason for your financial deficiency. Let's pinpoint any habits that are keeping you from your financial goals. You will be guided and encouraged to change your behavior and to overcome any barriers that may exist. You will then learn to control your spending and successfully manage your budget by using these 7 simple fruits. Are you ready? Ok, turn the page.

> *"And will you succeed? Yes! You will, indeed! (99 and ¾% guaranteed)"* ~ Dr. Seuss

Budgeting

Your Commitment

If you do not have a budget or do not feel the need for a budget, you are not alone. Many families do not follow a monthly budget although most of them struggle to pay their bills. They simply do not understand the benefits of budgeting.

Before we look at why many people avoid budgets, let's examine the question: What is a Budget? A budget is a spending plan. It is a mathematical equation: Income – Expenses = Spending Plan. It does not require an accounting degree, and it is not complicated. What it does require is commitment. You must keep track of your spending. Envisioning your dreams will make it easier to achieve your dreams. People that use budgets have a deeper yearning for a better and wealthier future. They are disciplined, and they consistently work towards their goals. They are also capable of distinguishing their needs from their wants. You must realize that all of us have things that we want, and we deserve many of them. The problem comes when we confuse the two and do not prioritize our spending.

A budget is the foundation of financial wellness. It is impossible to save or manage your spending without a budget. Your budget tells your money where it belongs. More importantly, it tells you how much money you have, how much you will need, and how you are spending that money. Each of your coins should have a purpose, and a budget provides a flowchart of how your money is received (income) and how the money is dispersed (spent). A few days after payday, have you ever thought: *I just got paid, where's the money?* A budget helps you to identify any financial leaks. It will show you if you are spending money unnecessarily. It also does something that you may not expect: it can bring peace into your home by eliminating sleepless nights filled with money worries. As you become more accountable, you will be calmer and at ease.

There are four primary purposes of money... to save, spend, invest, and to give; and, it all starts with a budget.

Let's look at common reasons for not having a budget:

I do not have time

Some people think that budgets are a long, complicated process. However, if you are already paying your bills, then you have time for a budget. A budget can simplify your life by telling you how to spend your money. Instead of worrying about if you can pay a bill, you will just pay it on the due date.

There is not enough money

Budgeting is about telling your money where to go. We are not talking about creating or adding another expense. It is about being respectful of your money. It is financially irresponsible to earn money and to be clueless about your spending. You might as well just throw it out of a window. Budgeting has absolutely nothing to do with the *amount* of money that you earn. It has everything to do with what you are doing with what you've earned. Regardless of your income or lack of income, there is no amount too small to budget. Start where you are. If you are a student, for example, you can still be accountable. If you receive money for special occasions such as birthdays and holidays, you must decide how to spend the money. (Hey, that's a budget!)

In the summer of 1980, as a pre-college student in the Upward Bound program, I received a $7.50 weekly stipend. This money represented more than just an allowance for me; it relieved me from being a broke college student. It prevented me from getting stranded without gas money (gas was about $1.20 a gallon), and it also encouraged me to save. Each week we received a crisp five-dollar bill, 2 one-dollar bills, and a shiny fifty-cent piece. As a teenager, I instinctively tucked away a few coins for a rainy day. I saved 50 cents per week. I carefully spent the balance because even back then $28 a month wasn't a lot of money. As my finances changed, so did my budget as shown in the upcoming pages. Yours will change too as your circumstances change, and it will require that you make revisions. As your income increases, you'll need to modify your budget. The more money that you earn, the more money that you could potentially spend. Therefore, even for those that are wealthy, a budget is a necessity. Many affluent families still practice budgeting as a means of maintaining their wealth.

It is too restrictive

Many people feel that they work every day, and do not want a budget dictating their lifestyle. It is viewed as a ball and chain, holding them down and preventing them from doing as they choose. To the contrary, a budget is like a roadmap; it shows you where to go. It ensures that you have allotted money for necessities as well as pleasures.

You dictate your budget. Remember, it is *your* budget. You are the one designing the plan. Yeap, it's yours… for better or for worse.

I will spend it anyway

Having a budget does not stop you from spending. It gives you a map so that you won't get lost in your spending journey. It provides you with an action plan and a strategy for spending your dollars. As your lifestyle changes, a budget must be revisited and adjusted. But, consistency is the key. There will be times that you will get slack, but you must get back on track and make appropriate spending decisions. When you were learning to ride a bike, after the first fall, did you give up? How many times did you fall? I remember constantly falling. Did I give up? No, I kept trying, and I am sure that you did too. Use the same resilience that you had as a child.

Yes, you will spend the money anyway. Why not have a plan to help you spend it more purposefully and aide you in setting boundaries? No more excuses! You must make a change. Commit yourself to a better financial future. Sign the below commitment:

I, _____, want to become financially fit. I will complete the exercises in this book and practice the Fruits beginning on _____/_____/20_____.

"We fall down, but we get up!" ~ *Donnie McClurkin*

My budget in the early years

When I was growing up, I witnessed my mother sitting at the kitchen table surrounded by a stack of papers and her checkbook. She had a list of everything that needed to be paid, and she would pay the bills accordingly. I never gave it much thought. It didn't seem as though she was doing anything noteworthy. I didn't think that she was unknowingly teaching me a valuable lesson. We were poor, and I would regularly hear her say that we were living paycheck-to-paycheck. I automatically assumed that budgeting from one paycheck to the next was a hardship. However, I often wondered how we were able to afford small luxuries. As po' as we were, we did take an occasional mini-vacation. I later learned that if you are budgeting and have emergency savings, you are technically not living paycheck-to-paycheck. If you have some money saved, even if it is a small amount, you can tide yourself over until the next paycheck. For those that choose not to save, they will eventually struggle.

Each time you receive some money, write down how it will be spent. Although I did not always do this, I have always understood the importance of accounting for every cent. I graduated from college and got married at an early age. I later divorced and moved back home. I was 25 years old, working part-time, and I had little debt and no responsibility. I "needed" a lot of things. I bought pocketbooks, clothes, shoes, and jewelry. I bought a lot of stuff!

Below is a sample of my budget:

$230	Car Payment (Nissan Sentra, in case you are wondering)
$100	Savings
$25	T.J. Maxx Layaway
$45	Kay's Jewelry Layaway
$35	Belk
$75	JCPenney
$75	Gas
$70	Miscellaneous (snacks, movies, eating out, club)
$655	Total

If you are questioning the budget, my only excuse is that I was young with no real responsibility. Nevertheless, I fully understood the concept, and I executed it. I jotted down my expenses, including monies spent on small items, such as snacks from the vending machines. This enabled me to account for miscellaneous items (cake, magazines, and the admission fee at the Nightclub) and kept tabs on my spending habits. Eventually, I was able to lump my miscellaneous cost together and stay within that range.

Should you write down every item that you buy? Once your spending pattern is revealed, your expenses can be narrowed down and categorized into the miscellaneous category. Tracking your expenses takes only a few minutes. It takes more time to check your social media accounts. Don't stress it. It may be uncomfortable at first, and you will get a lot of flak from your friends. My friends called me "cheap" and all sorts of names. They made occasional snide remarks about my money management until I lost my job. Once they witnessed that I was able to survive and sustain myself after the job loss, they were amazed. Once you start budgeting, you will see the benefits and eventually – so will your family and friends!

"Criticism is like water. Let it wash you, not drown you." ~ Unknown

How to begin

The first step is to examine your relationship with money. By completing the exercise below, you will discover the reasons for your money habits. If you have an unhealthy mindset, you'll continue to be broke and confused. You must identify the problem. For example, are you a shoe hoarder? Through this exercise, you may realize that as a child you had to wear your sister's hand-me-down shoes and you unconsciously decided that as an adult you were going to have as many shoes as you wanted. Or, perhaps you only shop when you are feeling sad. Shopping could remind you of happier times. Or maybe you feel inadequate if you don't have a new outfit for an event. On the surface, these actions mean nothing. But these are not superficial questions. Your past could be influencing your behavior and resulting in activities that leave you wondering why your money disappears. Your feelings, thoughts, and financial beliefs begin as a child. These feelings determine how you feel about money and how you relate to money. Therefore, you must dive deep within and seriously examine your motivations. Only then will you make a change by accepting the answers that you discover. The statements and questions on the next page will help you to identify your feelings.

1. As a child, I had as many toys as my friends.
2. My family was considered impoverished or needy.
3. I worked to support my family.
4. We didn't always have enough food to eat.
5. My family was financially comfortable or well-off.
6. My family lived on a budget.
7. Did your friends live in a beautiful home?
8. Did your neighbors go on vacations but your family didn't?
9. Were you unable to go to events with your friends?
10. Did you have considerably more than your friends?
11. Did your parents fight about money?
12. Did you receive an allowance?
13. We donated to our Church on a regular basis.
14. Did you get money as a gift for birthdays and holidays?
15. Was there a variety of food available to eat?
16. Were you ashamed to invite a guest to your home?
17. My parents never discussed money.
18. As a child, we were evicted from our home.
19. We frequently donated items to persons in need.
20. Our family owned a vacation or second home.

There are no right or wrong answers. But you will notice that your answers will be similar. My responses showed that although I did not grow up in a third world country, money did not flow freely at my house. Contrary to a friend of mine, I did grow up receiving new clothes, and I did not have to constantly wear hand-me-downs or second-hand clothes. Joan was raised by a single mother in a household with several siblings. As a teenager, I gave her my clothes, and she altered them to fit her (then) petite frame. She admits that this experience leads her to overspend. She does this to compensate for the financial hardships that she experienced as a teen.

Just as our childhood experiences shaped our visions and defined our decisions, your spending habits are reflective of your experiences. This exercise should shed some light on your behaviors. It identifies the origin of your feelings and reveals your earliest lessons on how money works. Seeing your experiences in black and white may provide you with an "ah-ha" moment. But do not be surprised if your overspending has nothing to do with a deprived childhood though. It could be that your parents were deprived, and their lack caused them to buy extra for you. You inherited the overspending gene. Perhaps after completing the exercise, you have realized that some of your actions are guilt-based because as a child your family had more than other families. This could explain why you overspend buying for others. Or, your actions could be based on your family's lack of funds. Whatever the reason, after you have looked at your money motivators, you will better understand your current financial circumstances. As you move forward, identify your goals and have faith that you *will* experience a financial breakthrough!

Asking why?

Since you are on a learning journey, let's examine your reasons for wanting a budget. Are you tired of your current situation? Do you want to be an example for your children? Whatever your reason, write it down. Writing down goals guarantees success. Write it down and put it somewhere so that you can see it. It will reinforce your goals and serve as a daily reminder. Another way to hold yourself accountable is to get an *accountability partner*. Select someone that will keep you on track. You will want someone that's firm and stern, someone that will say: "You have been slacking, you need to stop what you are doing (spending) and get it together (save)."

If you are married, your spouse should be your accountability partner. It can be a problematic relationship if you do not have the same overall goals. For example, if both spouses have an intention of buying a house or paying off their mortgage, they will be better partners. If one spouse's goal is to buy a new car, while the other spouse concentrates on the house, it is counterproductive. It will not work, and it may lead to financial infidelity or divorce. In case you are unfamiliar with the term financial infidelity, let me briefly explain. Financial infidelity is when a married person keeps money secrets from their spouse. It is financially unfaithful. An example of cheating is hiding your credit card balance or having a secret bank account. Let me jump in right here and say that it is okay to have separate bank accounts, and it is alright to have individual credit cards. What is agreed upon between spouses is good, just be sure not to jeopardize your spouse's financial health. Ok, back to budgeting...

To ensure that you and your partner are on the same page, individually make a list of your goals prioritizing them beginning with essential items. Next, create a combined list making sure that you prioritize all identical goals. Go through the remaining items and jointly decide on its importance. Some things will be immediate goals, and others will be long-term goals of five years or more. Lastly, use the templates provided to create a budget that addresses your combined goals, and caters to what works for both of you.

Notes

RoslynLash.com

Kindness

Reducing Stress

The word *kindness* is described as having a good spirit, doing nice things with a special emphasis on service. This chapter is about being kind to others and being kind to yourself by making good choices. The purpose of money is to save, spend, invest and give. Acts 20:35 teaches us that we are more blessed to give than to receive. You are blessed when your job gives you a 3% raise. So, why not give some or all of it to someone less fortunate? Many employers make it easier to donate by offering payroll deduction for donations to charitable organizations. Regardless of your income, you can contribute. No gift is insignificant or too small. All acts of kindness should be judged on the value of the giver's intent, on its merit.

This brings me to another point. We must also be kind to ourselves. We place ourselves in unkind situations, such as indebtedness. A brief example, if we have our hearts set on a 1-carat ring, we'll be horribly disappointed if we can only afford a ½ carat. To make ourselves feel better, we will buy the 1-carat ring with a credit card and then struggle to make the payments. Stop the nonsense and become financially conscious! Be truthful to yourself and accept that you cannot afford it. Accepting your current situation will aid you in making wise financial decisions.

Needs versus wants

You must identify your *needs* and *wants* as well as exercise some self-control. It is easy to confuse the two by misreading your feelings. Our needs are fundamental. We need food, shelter, water, and clothing. We become confused when we decide that we need Filet mignon instead of Salisbury steak, or we need a 5-bedroom house for our family of three, or we need designer clothes instead of clean, neat, non-designer clothes. This issue is especially apparent when we buy a car. We are intrigued by large, expensive cars. I can understand, they are beautiful. However, the question remains: *Is a luxury car a need?* In some cities, even a car may not be necessary. New York City, for example, has an extensive train system. Most people take alternate forms of transportation including cycling, walking, train, bus, or taxis. If you do not live in a metropolitan city, perhaps owning a car is a need, but owning a luxury car... well, that's a want. And, that is ok. Buying a luxury car is terrific if you can afford it, and it doesn't cause you financial hardship. If you have paid your bills and have contributed toward your long-term goals such as mortgage, savings, and retirement, and you still have money left over, and you want a luxury car, buy it --- buy whatever you want. After all, you have earned it, you deserve it, and more importantly, you can afford it!

When I was younger, I loved designer handbags. Regardless of the designer, if it had an impressive emblem, I bought it. I wanted at least one bag of every popular brand. My mom once commented, "I'll bet that you don't have as much money *in* the bag as you paid *for* the bag." Well, she was right. I barely had $20, but I'd paid nearly ten times that amount. Now that I am older and wiser, if I like a bag, and it is reasonably priced, I do not care about the label. It is more important that I have money *in* my purse.

It is important to scrutinize your *wants* and to also look carefully at what motivates you. Do you want an expensive pair of shoes because you love them, or do you want them because they are fashionable, your friend has a pair, or you want to impress your colleagues? If this is your motivation, and you continue with this line of thinking, you will remain broke. You need a mindset change. You must realize that you cannot have *everything* at once. Understand that I did not say that you cannot have what you want, you just can't have it *simultaneously*. Decide on the items that are most important to you and work responsibly toward buying those items. Using your credit card is not a responsible method of spending. As Romans 12:12 (GW) states, "Be happy in your confidence, be patient in trouble, and pray continually." Therefore, you must exercise patience and when possible, pay with cash. Below is a list of some basic needs and wants. There is also space for you to include your personal needs and wants. Be sure to complete this exercise; it will unconsciously help you when making purchases.

<u>Needs</u>	<u>Wants</u>
Housing	~~Cable~~ Streaming Device
Car	New Car
Food	Eating out
Clothes	New Clothes
Gas	Home Decor
Phone	Landline phone
Internet	Gifts
Medical	Movies
Toiletries	Jewelry

I was conflicted about placing the internet under the *needs* category. But, I realized that the internet is our way of connecting to the world. The World Wide Web is the information highway. It provides us with knowledge and access to information and learning tools. In fact, many of you are reading this on an electronic device connected to the internet. The internet provides a way of connecting, communicating, and sharing. I have provided you with several websites that you can use to implement your budget, and without the internet, it would be impossible. So yes, I categorized it as a need. If your life would suffer if you did not have an item or service, it is a need. Not having the internet could negatively impact your life.

On the chart below, you can list your needs and wants. This exercise will improve your decision-making skills. Having a clear mind is essential when preparing your budget. It is especially important if you are forced to eliminate some expenses.

Your needs and wants:

Needs	Wants

Sometimes the lines get blurry when distinguishing the difference between *needs* and *wants*. It is especially hard if the item is something that you need, and there is an expensive upgraded version that you would prefer. For example, if you live in an area of the country that is plagued with several feet of snow, you may need boots. The dilemma occurs when you see a pair of designer boots for $125 more than the non-designer brand. It is especially difficult when you can afford the designer boots. I know that *sometimes* you've gotta have things that are not needs. If those boots put a smile on your face and they are "must have" boots, admit that it is not a need and buy them. (This should not happen frequently.) Be sure to decide on what adjustments you will make to recoup the $125.

Living beneath your means

Stress-free living requires you to live below your means. What does this mean? It means to live on less money than you earn. For example, if there are two apartments and both units are safe, clean and decent, you would choose the least expensive unit. The extra money that you would have paid in rent can be deposited into your savings account. A similar example would be deciding between two same-size houses. The bank states that you can qualify for the higher priced home. It has impressive amenities, but you have no plans to use them. Why pay for features that you will not use? Therefore, you decide on the lower priced home (that you love equally as much) without the added features. Living beneath your means requires you to exercise your common sense and adjust your lifestyle. It is a small adjustment with a big reward.

"The opposite of more is enough." ~ William Paul Young, Author

Keeping up with the Joneses

Do not try to keep up with the Joneses. You do not know the Jones' situation. Mr. and Mrs. Jones may have thousands of dollars in credit card debt. Nerdwallet reports that in mid-2017, the average family had $16,883 in credit card debt. If that's an average figure, Mr. and Mrs. Jones may have $30,000 in *credit card* debt. And, that's not counting their other debts. Do you want to keep up with them? Be honest about *your* finances. What has put your funds in a rut? Are there any habits that you could adjust that would provide a brighter future?

You should analyze and prioritize your *wants*. Consider your jewelry, sports memorabilia, handbags, and even where you choose to live. Do you need to live in a complex that has a clubhouse? If you have a pool, do you use it? Do you need a fireplace? Could you save an extra $95 per month in a unit that doesn't have these amenities? Be kind to yourself by exercising self-control, acknowledging your wants, and then buying what you truly can afford. Ramit Sethi said it best in his book *I Will Teach You To Be Rich*, "*Spend on what you love. Frugality isn't about cutting your spending on everything. Frugality, quite simply, is about choosing the things you love enough to spend extravagantly on, then cutting cost mercilessly on the things you don't love. It's about making your own decisions about what's important enough to spend a lot on, and what's not, rather than blindly spending on everything. The problem is that hardly anyone is deciding what's important and what's not....*" Confusing your *wants* with your *needs* will lead to poor decisions and cause stress. Remember, saying NO to some of your wants means that you are saying YES to your future and your goals!

Several years ago, I worked as a Homeownership Coordinator and Loan Officer. I was responsible for screening Downpayment Assistance applications for first-time home buyers. I frequently saw people with cars that they could not afford. Approximately half of the applicants were denied because of high car payments.

The other half were dismissed due to poor credit. I will address credit in more detail later. You must prepare for your future by prioritizing your needs. It is imperative. If you are under 30, you probably have not given much thought about the retirement years, right? *Right!* After all, you are young and fabulous (and probably broke too). Nevertheless, you should be disciplined enough to spend intentionally and make small adjustments to your budget so that you can start saving money. When you get a little older or start having children, you will see the benefits of these minor adjustments. Each change brings you closer to your goal of financial wellness. Prioritizing, adjusting, and sacrificing are wealth building tools. More importantly, it helps to create an emergency fund for unexpected expenses. I continuously address the importance of maintaining an emergency savings account. I experienced a job loss, but I kept a rainy-day fund. Life isn't always kind, and it doesn't stop throwing curve balls after one mishap. In my case, the job loss was one crisis, and my totaled car was another misfortune.

As I'm writing this chapter my arm is itching badly. An insect bit me. I didn't see it, but it was felt. (Ouch!) I do not know what ate me, but thus far, I have taken two types of antibiotics. Based on my progress, or maybe I should say lack of progress, I believe that I will be forced to get a third prescription. The cost of the last medicine was $50. If you don't have the funds, $50 is a lot of money. If you have no means of getting $50, it might as well be $5,000. Why am I telling you this? Even small financial decisions can impact your life. If you do not monitor your habits and put yourself in check, you will sabotage your ability to establish an emergency fund. And when an emergency does occur, you will feel like it is a $5,000 emergency instead of a $400 necessity. You will have to either charge the expense, borrow money from friends, or beg your family. Each of these options will lead to stress, and that is unkind.

> "Do not buy what you want and then beg for what you need."
> *~ Eunice Suber, my mother*

Analyzing your spending habits

My philosophy is *even if it's on sale, it's not a bargain if you can't afford it!* If you are a constant spender or you are constantly *missing* money, this statement should resonate with you. Some people buy things that they don't need just because it's on sale. For example, they will see a pair of shoes initially priced at $225 that are on sale for 40% off, and they can't resist saving $90. Seriously? If you don't buy the shoes, you will save $225!

Modifying your spending habits does not imply that you must deprive yourself. It means that you must be mindful of your spending. Remain alert and examine your motivations. It could be that you live above your means, you have excessive debt, or you are spending uncontrollably. Your actions will impact your future. The consequences of those seemingly small decisions can have long-term adverse effects. Creating a new mindset is essential. Once your priorities are adjusted, you will hear a little voice saying, "That is enough" when you're approaching the boundaries of overspending. If you ignore this voice of reason, it may become necessary to seek professional help.

An Accredited Financial Counselor (AFC®) will intensely review your financial situation and provide tools to assist in reshaping your attitudes and behaviors about money. Suggestions will be provided based on your goals. We are trained to develop a plan to negotiate financial barriers, to ease your fears, and to relieve your stress. You can locate an Accredited Financial Counselor at AFCPE.org.

A few ways to budget are to buy out-of-season items, visit thrift shops, and use coupons. Buying off season clothing is one of the best ways to save money. Summer clothes can be bought for up to 50% off the retail price if purchased at the end of the season. The same applies to fall and winter clothes.

In one of my youth classes, I suggested shopping at Thrift Shops. One of the students said, "No, people have worn those clothes!" I told him that the same could apply to new merchandise bought at non-thrift stores; therefore, wash all items before wearing.

It's not a bargain if you can't afford it – even if it's on sale.
~ Yours truly, Roslyn Lash

Developing a workable spending plan

Are you always worrying about money? If you can't sleep at night or are living paycheck-to-paycheck, developing a budget or a spending plan will provide you with clarity and peace of mind. Each of your dollars should have a home, a destination... whether that is to pay for utilities, phone, car payment, or to buy groceries. Miscellaneous expenses are another category of concern. Eventually, you will be able to allocate a lump sum for your miscellaneous spending. As you begin, track *every* penny to determine how much you are spending on odds/ends, small purchases like donuts, coffee, and office pool lottery tickets (keep an eye on this expense). Tracking your spending will also help to eliminate non-sufficient funds (NSF) fees, late fees, and unnecessary charges. Too often we spend small amounts of money without realizing that the coins add up to missing dollars. For example, if each workday you visit the local bagel shop and spend $4 per visit, that is $20 per week. It does not seem like much money until you realize that it is $80 per month or $1,040 per year. If you bought bagels and took them to work, you could use that money for a nice vacation.

"An unwritten goal is merely a dream." ~ Author unknown

Zack, my first client, had very little debt. He loved to socialize with his friends and spent nearly $500 per month at restaurants and bars. He is not alone. Food and eating out are challenges for many households. Zack is young, single, and earns around $65,000 per year. His goals were to buy a house and pay off his car, but his actions did not match his long-term goals. Based on his income, he would not qualify for downpayment assistance, so he would be looking at putting down around $10,000 for the home. He will need money to move (especially if he moves out-of-state), and for other expenses, such as utility connection fees. We developed a plan that reduced the restaurant visits and increased his homeownership fund. I have listed his cost below along with the recommended revised budget:

Expense	Current Cost	New Budget	Savings
Entertainment	$140	$70	$70
Dining Out & Alcohol	$550	$275	$275
Food	$135	$360	-$225
Total Savings			$120

I suggested that instead of going out each weekend, twice a month he should go to the ABC store, buy his favorite alcohol, and prepare a nice home-cooked meal.

Making a meal and having his special "drinky-drink" at home for just two weekends per month saved $275. Additionally, his entertainment typically consists of going to a weekly movie, and occasionally to a play. I suggested that he purchase a T.V. streaming device and go to the movies twice a month. This simple action cut this expense in half. Hmm, I wonder how his girlfriend adapted to the changes.

Anyway, he decided to save the extra money and his savings increased without a great deal of effort. He made a relatively small adjustment. He still goes out but not quite as often. His priorities shifted. Now that he is in tune with his goals, he is excited to watch his money grow.

Creating a budget is not about deprivation or stripping away your pleasure. A successful budget will focus on you… your goals and your dreams, and it brings those things closer to you. Budgeting is about making a conscious decision on how to spend your money and how it can have a positive impact on your lifestyle. Instead of unconsciously spending your money on everything, you will make an intentional decision on what you like most and buy it.

> *"Beware of small leaks; a small leak will sink a great ship."*
> *~ Benjamin Franklin*

Notes

RoslynLash.com

Goodness

Get Organized

The fruit of *goodness* allows you to decide what is right and what is practical for creating a successful spending plan.

As children, we learned the differences between good and evil, right and wrong. As we mature, it becomes more apparent. Good actions are helpful, beneficial, and lead to positive results. For example, when budgeting, organizational skills lead to opportunities to save. I am unorganized, so it is sometimes a challenge. I have purchased duplicate items such as cleaning, office, and personal supplies because I did not remember that I had already bought them. I have also missed out on rebates because I have neglected to mail the forms. I have learned to keep a calendar of financial dates.

Now, it is time to dig through your bills. Let's get started!

Budgeting requires documentation of your income and expenses. Your expenses include your cost of living expenses, such as utilities, food, and housing. It also includes debts, such as car payments, credit card payments, and other loans. Gather this information; you will need it when you start plugging in the numbers. Organizing your finances will help you set goals and assure that you pay your bills on time. Goodness is more than goal setting and organization. It also applies to maintaining a positive attitude. It is difficult to stay upbeat when unexpected expenses occur. When you think about how much money it takes to maintain your household it can become frightening. However, you must remain in prayer and ask God to direct your steps. You will then miraculously balance your attitude and your budget.

Setting goals

Goal setting is vital in your financial wellness journey. You should tweak your goals periodically as your lifestyle and circumstances change. You must also revisit your long-term budget if you have a change in income or your family size changes such as a birth or death. You especially need to modify your budget if you are overspending.

When making a budget, whether it is a new budget or a revised one, the commonly used acronym "SMART" is an excellent rule to follow. An example of a money-saving goal is:

S = Specific: I am going to save $500.

M = Measurable: I will save $100 toward this goal every month.

A = Achievable: I will carry my lunch to work twice a week.

R = Realistic: Instead of buying snacks from the vending machine, I will carry my treats.

T = Timely: This goal will be accomplished within five months.

Specific: Be precise. It will require that you detail as many of the 5 W's as possible: who, what, why, where, and when. Questions such as *"Who is involved? What do I want to accomplish? Why is this goal important? When will I begin the task?"* will make it easier to accomplish your goals.

Measurable: You must establish criteria to measure your progress. This is a measuring stick of sorts. This step tells you how far you have come and how far you must go to achieve your goals. If you have a 5-year goal, you must set benchmarks to plot your progress. You could measure your advancement in 6-month intervals, for example.

Achievable: You have listed your goals, and your next step is to figure out the best strategy to achieve them. You have examined your relationship with money, and you know which spending behaviors are beneficial. You should continuously analyze your needs and wants.

Realistic: Your goals must be realistic. If you needed to lose 20 pounds, you would not expect to lose it within a week. A fad diet will allow you to lose the weight in an unhealthy way. Just as you want to be physically healthy, you should also want to be financially healthy and wise. You cannot save $1,000 in a month if your earnings are $1,200 a month. At a minimum, you must pay for food and living expenses; so, this would not be a realistic goal.

Timely: You must set a timeframe for your goal. This timeframe should also be achievable and realistic. For example, some companies have an annual sale. This is the biggest deal of the year where prices are slashed. If your goal is to save $200, and you have one pay period before the sale, but your check is usually $250, you've set an untimely and unrealistic goal. You have other obligations and priorities, so this timeframe does not work.

Goals should be categorized based on projected achievement dates. Therefore, you will have short-term and long-term goals. Utilize the SMART steps for each goal. Short-term goals can be achieved within five years. If the target date is longer than five years, it is a long-term goal, and you should establish periodic check-ups to monitor your progress.

Common goals are:

Pay off mortgage	Contribute to a retirement fund
Pay off student loan debt	Purchase a car
Travel	Buy a House
Eliminate credit card debt	Build emergency savings

Goal 1:

Goal 2:

Goal 3:

"The plans of the diligent lead surely to abundance."
~ Proverbs 21:5 (ESV)

Notes

RoslynLash.com

Discipline

Pay Yourself First

This principle does not override your religious or spiritual commitment of paying tithes. It encourages you to save and to *"pay yourself first"* before you pay bills and before you withdraw money from your account. This simple rule is perhaps the most important financial lesson that you will ever learn. It is the foundation of financial wellness. It is the process of saving *before* you pay the rent, buy food, or pay your child's daycare bill. This attribute requires discipline, and it cultivates a sense of faith. Saving is hard because money seems to disappear like a thief in the night. Therefore, the best way to protect yourself from unhealthy spending habits is to have your savings automatically drafted from your paycheck *before* you allocate funds for other expenses. You can do this yourself, or you can set it up on an App, such as Digit. We will talk more about ways to save later.

The book *The Richest Man in Babylon* by George Samuel Clason is a classic story which addresses the age-old question: *"How do the rich get richer?"* If everyone has 24 hours in a day with relatively the same opportunities, why are some people rich while others are poor? Of course, there could be outstanding factors, such as discrimination, inherited wealth, and education. But, have you ever earned the same salary as your co-worker, and all other elements were the same, but they always had more money than you? The reason is that they understood the principle of paying themselves first. That is why you freaked out when the work hours were cut, but they weren't alarmed. They were prepared. When I worked at the airline, we experienced massive layoffs. As staff reductions were being announced, Tim was reading his newspaper. Management delivered the news as he continued to read.

He did not lift the paper to make eye contact or acknowledge the announcement. He was not fazed by the reduction in staff. Tim was a Real Estate Investor, and even if he lost his job, he would have an income. Am I suggesting that you become an investor? No, not necessarily. The message that I want to convey is the importance of preparation. Prepare for your future... your unforeseen future, and the best way to do that is to "pay yourself first."

If you worked full-time for an entire year and saved $1 for each hour worked, you should have at least $2080 (40 hours x 52 weeks) in a savings account. You must "pay yourself first." You pay the landlord or mortgage company, utilities and energy providers, cable, internet, and any other bills that land in your mailbox. Heck, some of you even have layaway that you regularly pay! You are responsible for your debts, and you must have the discipline to pay yourself. Currently, you value everyone else's right to be paid. You work hard, right? Then, you deserve to be paid too!

I hope that I have convinced you to "pay yourself first" and start saving. If so, the question becomes: *How much should I save?* This is a tricky question. The correct answer depends on your resources and financial situation. Below is a list of savings strategies that will fit into your budget regardless of your income. Rather than being overly concerned about an amount, just start!

> *"No discipline seems pleasant at the time, but painful. Later on, however, it produces a harvest of righteousness and peace for those who have been trained by it."* ~ Hebrews 12:12

Savings strategies for paying yourself

$1,000 Emergency Fund: This is the baby step in paying yourself first. If you don't have any cash reserve, telling you to save 15% or more of your income might feel like a stretch. Therefore, starting to save is more important than determining an amount. This goal is achievable by using mobile apps such as Digit, Qapital, and Chime, or the investment app Acorn. These apps automatically transfer money into your savings account or round up your purchases to the nearest dollar and deposit the balance into an account. Some of the apps are free while others charge a low monthly fee, but they are a terrific way to save.

Acorn:

This investment app works similar to the others except you are investing your money in various stocks and bonds. You must decide on your investment portfolio based on your risk level. Five portfolios range from Conservative to Aggressive. You can choose to be Conservative where you will experience less risk and less reward, you can decide on an Aggressive portfolio resulting in high risk and high rewards, or you can choose a collection somewhere in between. There's a wide range of choices based on your comfort level, and as of this writing, the service charge is only $1 per month for balances under $5,000.

Do you want $5 just for joining Acorn? Use the link https://acorns.com/invite/6679HA, and we will both get $5!

10% of your net (take home) income: For example, if you receive a bonus for $100, you should immediately transfer $10 into your savings account. It is best to make the transfer as soon as you receive extra money. If you wait, you will probably spend it.

If your income is solely from your job, and not from bonuses or commission checks, be sure to include 10% of your take-home pay in your budget.

15% of your gross income: This does not have to be an immediate savings goal. It is just your next step. (And before you get uncomfortable or pull out the calculator, the amount can be a combination of emergency plus retirement savings.) The simplest way to save is via Payroll Deduction. If your company offers a retirement such as a 401k, you can have a percentage of your income deducted from your check. For example, you can save 12% of your income toward savings, and contribute 3% of your income for retirement. If your employer offers a 401k retirement match, be sure to contribute up to the match amount. If you contribute 3%, many employers will match up to 6%. It is free money, so be sure to contribute enough to qualify for the full match.

Alternative form of retirement saving:

If you have a mortgage and your employer does not offer a pension match, or for whatever reason, you have chosen not to contribute to a retirement fund, consider prepaying your mortgage (making extra principal payments) as an alternate form of saving.

Most of your income, up to 50% in some unfortunate instances, goes toward housing expenses. Once this expense is eliminated, you won't need as much money for retirement. Reducing your debt will increase your cash flow. During the economic downfall of 2008, I used the money that I normally would have contributed to a 401k to prepay my mortgage. That proved to be a blessing once I lost my job.

You can save thousands of dollars and shave years off your mortgage term by making an extra principal payment each year. Some companies offer this service for a fee. Do not subscribe to this service. You can prepay the mortgage without hiring someone. Just decide on an amount, i.e., $25, $50, $125, or any amount that you choose, and pay it consistently. Be sure to check with your bank to be sure that your account is being properly credited.

20% or more of your Gross Income: It may not be easy to achieve this level of savings. I added it because just like no amount is too small to save, no amount is too significant either.

"Don't save what is left after spending; spend what is left after saving."
~ Warren Buffett

Methods of budgeting

There are several ways to track your spending. While one process of budgeting may be appropriate for you, it may not work for your partner. It is crucial that you find a method or a combination of techniques that mutually work for both of you. Regardless of the method(s) that you choose, there must be a system of checks and balances. You must know how much money is entering your household and how much is departing.

Envelope system

The envelope system is a cash-based budgeting method. It is a simple system where you put your money in a designated envelope for a specific bill. For example, each bill has an envelope... there's an envelope for rent, utilities, entertainment, food, gas, miscellaneous, etc. Users of this method quickly become aware of their spending habits. This cash-only system forces you to rethink your purchases. Unlike purchasing items on credit, you see and feel the money. Buying merchandise can be financially depressing when the envelope hits zero. Seeing your balance decrease keeps you from overspending. Unlike buying with a credit card, you immediately witness your declining balance.

Zero-based budget

The objective of a zero-based budget is to be accountable for every dollar. If there is extra money remaining after deducting your expenses from your income, you must adjust your budget to determine where the excess should be spent. If you have paid all your bills... short-term and long-term (property taxes and other irregular expenses), any extra money should be deposited into an emergency fund.

Budgeting tools

Several apps and websites help with budgeting such as Mint, EveryDollar, BudgetTracker, Prism, and PocketGuard. For a budgeting excel spreadsheet, visit RoslynLash.com and look under *forms*. Once you have downloaded it to your computer, you can begin inputting your data. You should also get a calendar so that you can track your paydays, due days of bills, and any other days that may affect your budget.

Combination of budgeting styles

Many people prefer to use a combination of budgeting methods by using a written or electronic budget for their essential bills. You may use the envelope system for expenses, such as entertainment and dining. The envelope will be used for expenses that will not impact your lifestyle. This does not mean that it is a free-for-all envelope. The purpose of the money is labeled on the envelope, and it should be used accordingly.

The budget on the next page is of a person with a net income of $2500 per month. Periodic expenses are identified with an asterisk (*) and in italics.

Note: Do not be concerned about the figures used in this example. Remember, this is just a sample. Your earnings and cost could drastically differ. What is important is that you learn how to prepare *your* budget. Besides, this example is based on a monthly budget. You must revisit your spending plan each payday. Also, do the same steps for any other monies that you receive. Whether you get a $20 or $300 bonus, or a $2,500 tax refund check, you must determine how the money will be spent.

Home	Cost
Rent/Mortgage	$700
Utilities	$130
Cell	$45
Internet	$60
Expenses	**Cost**
Food	$400
After School Childcare	$200
Transportation	**Cost**
Car Payment	$300
Gas & Insurance	$185
Car tags & title & inspection	*$17 ($200 per year)*
Property taxes	*$8 ($90 per year)*

Financial	Cost
Tithes	$250
Emergency Savings	$50
Credit Card #1	$25
Credit Card #2	$35
Loan #1:	$45
Travel Club	*$50*
Total Cost:	$2,500

Tip: Calculate the monthly cost for your variable expenses and deposit the cost into a separate account.

Based on the above budget, the variable expenses (listed in italic) have been converted to the monthly cost and transferred to the below periodic chart:

Variable bills- sample:

Type	Cost
Car tags & title & inspection	$17
Property taxes	$8
Vacation	$50
Variable Total Cost:	$75

In this example, all monthly variable expenses totaling $75 should be deposited into a separate savings account. This will eliminate payment shock when you receive the bills. Similarly, Christmas comes on the same date every year! The 25th of December is Christmas *every* year. If you celebrate this holiday, you should expect to buy gifts. There is no reason to be unprepared for periodic or variable expenses. In the above example, $50 is allocated for vacation. For many households, saving for vacation is impossible... not to mention impractical. If your income does not allow you to save for vacation, you must plan for it from other resources, such as your tax refund. Personally, it is not easy for me to plan a vacation. I usually do not know in advance where I am going, who will travel with me, or how much it will cost. I do most of my budgeting closer to the vacation date. I will save a little during the year and then use other funds to supplement the trip. Either method is fine. Remember, this is your budget! There is no right or wrong technique. When it comes to budgeting, the only error that you can make is not having one.

> *Tip: If you don't want to save monthly for a variable expense, you must use other funds, such as a bonus check or tax refund.*

DYOB: Doing your own budget

You have reviewed the sample budget, it is now time to prepare your personal budget. Again, right now, you are using the old method of paper and pencil. Once you are comfortable with the process, you can use an app such as Mint, EveryDollar, and BudgetTracker, Prism, and PocketGuard. There are various apps available. In Google, enter the words: *budgeting apps*.

You must know your take-home pay (net income) before you can develop a budget. You will need to include all sources of income below:

Salary or wages	Social Security
Child Support	Retirement i.e. 401k, 503b
Alimony	Pension
Commission	Dividends
Rental Income	Disability
Stocks, bonds, etc.	Other

Enter your income below:

Income	Source
Total: $	

The total income is the amount that you will use to prepare your budget.

Next, list each of your expenses. There is a comprehensive budget form in the Appendix that you can later use. It should capture all your expenses. For illustration purposes, we are going to use the slightly condensed version below. If there is an expense, such as your vehicle registration, which is paid yearly, divide the amount by 12 to calculate the monthly cost. You must save this amount per month. Variable expenses will cause you the most hardship. Why? It is easy to forget bills that are only paid once or twice a year. Below is a list of typical expenses. If you have one that is not listed, write it in the space provided:

Discipline: Pay Yourself First

Home	Cost
Rent/Mortgage	
* *Property Taxes & Insurance*	
Utilities	
Phone(s): Home & Cell	
* *Home repairs/maintenance*	
Other:	

Daily Expenses	Cost
Food	
Childcare	
Other:	

Transportation	Cost
Car Payment	
Other: Gas & Insurance	
* Car tags & title & inspection	
* Property taxes	
Other:	

Financial	Cost
Tithes	
Emergency Savings	
Credit Card #1	
Credit Card #2	
Credit Card #3	
Loan #1:	

Loan #2:	
Other:	
	Total Cost: $

The items listed in italics with an asterisk are periodic or variable expenses. Again, these are bills that you receive on an infrequent basis, such as quarterly, semi-annually, or once a year. You must calculate the yearly cost and divide that amount by 12 to determine the cost per month. For example, if you receive a $600 bill per year for your property taxes, you must allocate $50 each month toward this cost ($600/12=$50).

If you get paid every other week and would prefer saving from each check, use the below calculations:

You get paid	Divide the bill by
Weekly	52
Every Other Week	26
Twice a month	24
Monthly	12

If you are a part-time college student living at home with a yearly tuition bill of $3000 (I know that is ridiculously low, but indulge me), and you get paid every week, you would save $58 per week ($3000/52). If you received payment every other week, you would save $116 ($3000/26) each pay period. Keep in mind that getting paid every other week is not the same as getting paid twice a month. Receiving your check *every other week* means that you are paid 26 times a year. You will receive an extra check twice a year, usually in the Spring and the Fall.

If you are paid *twice a month* (typically on the 15th and 30th), it is 24 times per year. If you get confused, do not worry about it, just look at the above chart.

Regardless of how often you get paid, if you are short on discipline, you will also be short on money. Paying bills is challenging if you lack self-control. To make it easier, calculate the cost of your variable expenses and open a separate account for these costs. Transfer your variable expenses from your budget to the below chart:

Variable expenses	Cost
	Variable Total Cost: $

"Wisdom is knowing which path to take. Integrity is taking it."
~ M.H. McKee

Notes

RoslynLash.com

Patience

Credit Cards and Impulsive Spending

Since this book is about budgeting, I was not going to include anything about credit cards or debt management. I then realized that after paying your living expenses and all other budgeted items, what remains are credit cards, loans, and debts. Therefore, I would be remiss if I did not address credit and debt. After all, one of the primary reasons for budgeting is to eliminate these bills.

My first lesson about credit

My first introduction to credit was during my pre-teen years. I wanted a bicycle for Christmas. My mother told me that if I got the bike on Christmas day, I would have to get a store brand bike. But if I waited until after Christmas, just one day later, I could get a Schwinn. I do not recall why one day influenced her decision. If you are unfamiliar with the Schwinn brand, it was the bomb bicycle in the 1970s. It was *the* bike! Anyway, guess what I chose? You guessed it – the store brand bike. I just had to have a bike on Christmas day. As winter passed so did the newness of my bicycle. It was not a good bike. I complained to my mom, and she said, "I'm still paying on that bike." I was shocked. We were almost into the summer season, and she was still paying for a Christmas gift! How could that be true? That was my first lesson on two critical issues: being patient (I should have waited and gotten the Schwinn) and how interest rates work. Even at an early age, I knew that there was something wrong with continuously making payments - seemingly forever. Fortunately, credit card bills now show how long it will take to pay the balance completely. This provides a clue for how much you will pay over the life of the loan. Hopefully, I have convinced you to wait and rely more on cash for your purchases. Once you factor in the accumulated interest, the things that you buy probably aren't worth the total cost.

> *"The person who removes a mountain begins by carrying away small stones." ~ Chinese Proverb*

Advantages and disadvantages of credit

Financial responsibility means being reliable and exercising patience. Being patient may require that you delay purchases. There are advantages and disadvantages to having credit cards. Some of the benefits are as follows:

- Helps build credit
- Safer than cash when traveling (for hotels and car rentals)
- Reward points

Below are the disadvantages of owning a credit card:

- Encourages overspending
- High-interest rates
- Excessive fees

Additional advantages could be listed but, it is important to consider the weight and impact of each item. For example, having reward points may not be beneficial if the interest rate on the card is high. If the interest rate is 21%, it does not matter what perks or rewards (gas points, airline/travel miles) that you receive, it is just not worth it.

The overwhelming disadvantages of having a credit card are the Annual Percentage Rate (APR) and fees. Some cards have rates that are enormously high. Not all cards are unreasonable. Occasionally you can find a card with a low-interest rate. For example, if a card has an interest rate of 6%, your fee will be 6% of your balance each year. Think of it this way, for every $1 that you borrow; you will pay back an extra six cents. If the APR is higher, you will pay back more money. For a card with a high-interest rate of 29% for example, for every $1 that you borrow you will pay an extra 29 cents.

At an interest rate of 29%, if you borrow $1, you will repay $1.29. That is ridiculous! The interest is nearly one-third of the amount borrowed. A high-interest credit card requires you to pay more money, which means it will take longer to pay off the card. Remember: higher interest = more money = longer term. The reverse is also true. A low-interest card requires less money which shortens the repayment term.

Tip: Credit card perks do not matter if you are paying a high-interest rate!

The cost of credit

When you borrow money or use credit cards, it is not free. You receive the convenience of using the credit card, but you WILL pay. The trick is to spend as little money as possible. There are costs associated with credit card usages. Interest is a cost that lenders charge for letting you use the card. Interest rates can vary drastically. It is not uncommon to see fees from around 7% to nearly 30%. Many people view these percentages as just numbers. I am here to tell you that they are not merely numbers. These numbers can affect your bottom line. The difference between paying 7% and 21% can add up to thousands of dollars over the life of the loan. It can make an enormous difference in your wallet.

It is important to understand how high-interest rates will affect your debts as well as your investments. A high percentage rate is terrible for your debts but great for your investments.

Lisa understood how interest rates work. Lisa and Gina are best friends. They were next door neighbors, they went to the same school, and they were college roommates. The mountains were visible from their dorm, and they made plans to rent a cabin and take a hike in the mountains. After graduation, it was time to take the trip. Both opened credit cards and each charged $1,000. The interest rate on Lisa's credit card was 12%. She faithfully paid her bill each month making the minimum payment of $15. Years after Lisa's card was paid she asked Gina about taking another trip. Gina said that she could not afford it because she was still paying for the first trip. Lisa was shocked; that trip was nearly ten years ago.

Let me illustrate the difference in monthly payments as well as the cost of two interest rates:

> Lisa: Her $1,000 credit card balance at 12% APR took 8.25 years to pay off. She made a payment of 2% of the balance, not less than $15 per month. Her total cost was $1,545, she paid $545 in interest ($1545 - $1000).
>
> Gina: Her $1,000 credit card balance at 21% APR takes 19.6 years to pay off. She is making a payment of 2% of the balance, not less than $15 per month. Like Lisa, she has never been late, but her total cost is $3,798. She paid $2,798 in interest ($3,798 - $1,000).

A minimum payment of $15 was required for both cards. But there is a 9% difference in the rate between the two credit cards, and their total cost reflects that difference. Lisa, the informed cardholder, had the lower rate of 12% and she paid $2253 ($2798-$545) less in interest. Gina's interest rate is 21%. Consequently, Gina paid for that one vacation for nearly 20 years! I hope that her pictures were awesome. Twenty years is a long time to pay for a trip, a souvenir keychain, or a T-shirt.

> *"We begin as fools and become wise through experience."*
> *~ African Proverb*

The benefits of having good credit

You can expect a better interest rate if you have a good credit score. The reason that Lisa's interest rate was 12% and Gina's rate was 9 points higher at 21% is because Lisa had a higher credit score. Can you believe that a lower score could cost you thousands of dollars? Yup, Gina's lower score cost her over $2200! The below table breaks down a monthly mortgage payment for a $150,000, 30-year fixed rate mortgage based on the credit score.

FICO® Score	Annual % Rate	Monthly Payment
760-850	4.149%	$729
700-759	4.371%	$749
680-699	4.548%	$764
660-679	4.762%	$784
640-659	5.192%	$823
620-639	5.738%	$874

http://www.myfico.com/LoanCenter/Mortgage/ as of March 26, 2018

The above chart shows the principal and interest payments (excluding taxes and insurance) for people with excellent to average scores. The table does not include rates for lower scores. Although scores may vary between the three agencies (Equifax, TransUnion, and Experian), scores generally range from 300 to 850. Scores ranging between 619-580 are considered weak. Scores ranging from 579-500 are considered bad, and scores below 500 are viewed as horrible. Notice that there is a difference of $145 between a person with an 850 score versus a person with a 620 score. It is the same house! Lisa, the homeowner with the higher credit score, could afford her home and still have an extra $145. Of course, someone with a score under 620 would have an even higher mortgage payment. Had Gina been approved, her mortgage payment would be more expensive.

Your credit matters, and it pays to be in the *700 club*. A poor credit score will affect your life. It can even affect your employment. Many employers will check your credit report. Signing a release form authorizing them to do a background check could include a credit check. Also, when you are applying for an apartment, your credit may be checked. Landlords want to know if you can pay and if you are willing to pay. Your paystubs will show your ability, but your credit report shows your willingness.

> *"He who asks a question is a fool for five minutes; he who does not ask remains a fool forever." ~ Chinese Proverb*

Notes

RoslynLash.com

Love

Money and Relationships

Have you ever wondered why Flight Attendants suggest that in case of an emergency, you should place the oxygen mask over your face before helping others? It is because you cannot help others if you are unconscious. Likewise, before you can truly love someone else, you must love thyself first.

Your credit history can affect your love life. *US News & World Report* conducted a study which showed that 9 out of 10 survey respondents said financial responsibility was important when considering a partner. That is 90% of those surveyed. Hmm, maybe they are onto something. Perhaps there is a correlation between one's level of commitment in a relationship and their level of financial responsibility.

Having a loving relationship without money worries is the goal of most people. Giving and receiving love is a basic need. Love is the core of our being. It is not surprising that many people turn to matchmaking and online dating services. Many have found true love while others have become victims of a con artist. These con artists are masters of deception and skilled at swindling money, your money! If you are developing a new relationship, beware of these red flags:

- Frequently asking for money
- Waiting for a BIG opportunity or a large check
- Cannot pay their bills
- Does not work or has questionable employment
- Discreet about their finances or job status

- No money for entertainment
- Uses emotional blackmail (If you love me you would...)

Having financial issues is not shameful. It is only disgraceful when someone pretends to love another while breaking hearts, stealing money, and destroying lives. The pain of being taken advantage of is not limited to lovers, however. Parents, children, and other family members can also be guilty of scheming to take your hard-earned money. And you, at least some of you, are enablers. You allow healthy, non-disabled individuals to repeatedly *"borrow"* money, even though they live more extravagantly than you. They buy expensive clothes, travel, eat at fancy restaurants, and pamper themselves in ways that you cannot afford. Yet, you give them money. (Crazy, huh?)

Pam and Brenda inherited their parent's house. Pam and her husband own a home, and they have two children. One child recently graduated from college, and the younger child will soon be a freshman. Brenda is a working divorced mother. She is raising her children with financial assistance from her ex-husband. Since Pam already has a house, she agreed to let Brenda live in their parent's home. When Pam contacted me, she had some financial concerns. She and her husband weren't having any significant hardships, but they needed a second opinion since college tuition was a continuous part of their budget. After analyzing their finances, I noticed that their home maintenance costs were excessively high. I questioned her, and she revealed that the repairs were for the family's home aka Brenda's home. Each time the house needed something (roof, refrigerator, property taxes and insurance), Brenda called Pam. Let me reiterate that Brenda has a job and she lives rent free – and Pam pays for the upkeep! Apparently, in this type of situation, Pam hasn't learned to say NO. Pam, who has good intentions, is an enabler. She is being used, and she is permitting Brenda to avoid responsibility. Being single does not give Brenda permission to discount Pam's budget. Pam had the following maintenance cost:

	Amount spent	*minus* Pam's	Savings
Taxes	$2100	$1200	$900
Insurance	$1100	$500	$600
Roof	$3800	$0	$3800
Appliances	$800	$0	$800
Total	$7800		

Over the course of 18 months, Pam spent a total of $7800 on housing-related expenses. Most of the cost was for Brenda's home because Pam's expenses only cost $1700 ($1200 + $500) for taxes and insurance. Allowing Brenda to stand on her own feet would save Pam $6100 ($7800 - $1700). Pam, being a sweetheart, was concerned about how Brenda would survive without her help. I explained that since Brenda is not paying rent she can afford to pay the housing expenses. Brenda's cost was $6100 over 18 months. If she saved just $339 per month ($6100/18) she would have enough to cover the taxes and insurance. She would also have a reserve for unexpected expenses. Contributing $339 per month is a small amount to pay for shelter.

We must give to those that are sick, disabled, elderly, or truly in need. If this was Brenda's case, not only would I expect for Pam to help, but I would encourage her. Galatians 6:2 states that we should carry each other's burdens. In this situation, Brenda is not carrying her weight. Instead, she is acting like a parasite.

If you are in a similar situation, you must learn to say NO (com'on say it right now). Do not be an enabler. Enabling is not love. NO – that is your answer. No further explanation is required.

"...faith, hope, and love. But the greatest of these is love."
~ 1 Corinthians 13:13

Whole love but divided bills

Many loving couples use unloving ways to divide and pay their bills. In the below example, David earns $4,500 per month, and Nancy earns $3,500 monthly. It would be disproportionately unfair to split the bills 50/50. Since Nancy earns less, she should pay less toward the bills. It is not fair to overwhelm David either. Therefore, it is best to use a percentage-based contribution amount. If their total household income is $8,000 ($4500 + $3500), this figure will be used to determine their percentages.

Monthly Income	$8,000
Monthly Bills	$5,000

David's Income	$4,500		Nancy's Income	$3,500
Divided by Total Income	$8,000		Divided by Total Income	$8,000
As % of Income	56%		As % of Income	44%

David should be responsible for paying 56% ($4500/$8000) of the bills, and Nancy will pay the remaining 44% of the bills. Since the total monthly bills are $5,000, David will pay $2,800 ($5000 x 56%) each month. Nancy is responsible for the balance of $2,200 ($5000 x 44%).

Notes

RoslynLash.com

Faithfulness

Your Credit Score Matters

I am frequently asked about establishing or rebuilding credit. It is an important question because having credit is almost a necessity. In an ideal world, we could pay for everything in cash. That is the objective. In the meantime, we must establish and maintain our credit faithfully. Being faithful means being true to your word and accepting your responsibility. We use our credit to purchase high dollar items such as furniture, cars, and houses, and we must be accountable and financially responsible for repaying our creditors on time and as agreed.

How Credit Is Determined:

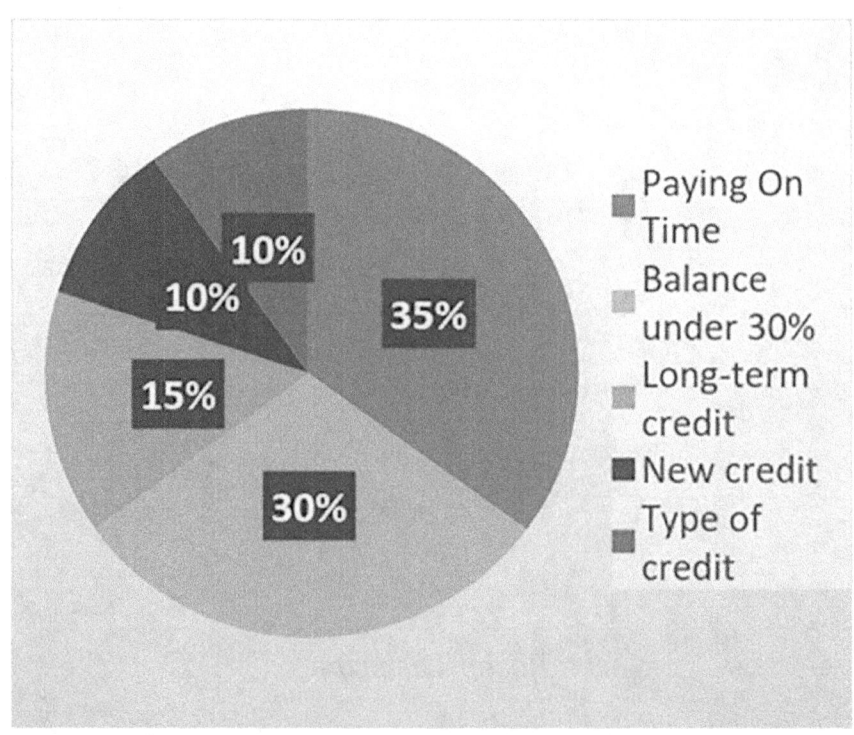

The previous chart demonstrates the primary criteria used in establishing credit scores per Fair Isaac and Company at myFICO.com. The three credit scoring agencies (Equifax, TransUnion, and Experian) use different algorithms to calculate the scores. Each agency's rating may differ from the other agencies. However, the score is a 3-digit number typically ranging from 300 – 850 where a score of 700 is considered good. This score helps creditors determine your creditworthiness. Each lender sets its scoring system, but the higher the score, the more likely you will be approved for a loan. A higher score indicates that you are financially responsible and are a lower financial risk.

Here is a breakdown of the factors that a credit score is composed of:

- **35% On-time payments:** Paying your bills on time is the best way to establish and maintain good credit. Paying on time tells the creditors that you are faithful and reliable to your debts.
- **30% Utilization Rate:** The words utilization and utilize means *to use*. To maintain a low utilization rate, you must keep your balances low. The amount of debt that you have compared to the amount of available credit determines the utilization rate. Therefore, keep balances less than 30% of your credit limit. For example, if your credit limit is $700, you should not carry a balance of more than $210.
- **15% Long Term Credit:** This factor considers how long you've had an account. An aged account provides more history for analyzing. If you can maintain credit for an extended period, you can successfully manage your finances.
- **10% New Credit:** The amount of new credit in your credit portfolio plays a role in your score. Each time you apply for new credit, your credit report generates what is known as a Hard Inquiry. The higher the inquiries, the

lower your credit score. Multiple inquiries give the impression that you are desperate. Therefore, it is best to minimize new accounts.

- **10% Type of Credit:** This factor looks at your accounts to see if you have a diverse mixture of credit. A good balance would include an installment account, such as a car payment or mortgage, and a revolving account, such as a credit card.

The most popular way to maintain or improve your credit is by paying your bills ON TIME. *On Time* is defined as *on or before* the due date. Although it may not immediately show on your credit report, your bill is considered late if paid after the due date. Delinquencies remain on your report for up to seven years. A low credit score and a bad payment history will keep you from making high dollar purchases.

Jim always dreamed of buying a two-story house. He visualized purchasing a home with a basement so that he could have a "man-cave."

He had minimal debt, he had recently paid off his truck, and he did not have any credit cards. He also had a solid work history. It sounds like homeownership was a slam dunk for him, right? No, it was not easy. Jim had not made his truck payment or his credit card payments on time. He didn't think that it mattered since they would eventually have zero balances.

Below is a chart showing Jim's bills and a history of his payment dates:

Account	% Rate	Payment	Due Date	Date Paid
Loan	13%	$25	Sep 3	Oct 13
Truck	8%	$305	Sep 10	Oct 13
Rent	0%	$805	Oct 1	Oct 05
Visa #1	15%	$108	Oct 13	Nov 22
Visa #2	17%	$75	Oct 15	Nov 22

Jim paid his bills over 30 days late, and that lowered his score. He assumed that since the two Visas were paid off in November, his credit would not be affected. However, that hurt his credit score. He also thought that paying his rent within the grace period would overshadow the delinquent credit card bills. He certainly did not expect it to hinder him from qualifying for a mortgage. Paying his rent on time was his wisest decision. Make sure that you always have a place to stay at (not grammatically correct, I know). Banks determine your qualifications by analyzing your income, debts, and payment history. Lenders will scrutinize your payment history twelve months prior to your loan application. Since most of Jim's bills were late, his dream of homeownership was postponed. He started paying his bills on time, and his credit score increased by several points. He was later approved for a loan, and he became a homeowner.

Tip: Minimizing your debt and paying your bills on time accounts for approximately 65% of your credit score.

Notes

Joy

The Pleasure of Reducing Debt

Are you wondering how *joy* applies to your money? You must receive more pleasure from reducing debt and saving money than you do from spending. Let me say it another way, you must enjoy saving more than you do spending. Once this mindset is developed, you will take immense pleasure in saving money. Taking your weekly trips to the mall will have less appeal. You will be joyous when you see your credit card balances drop and your savings account increase.

When determining how much personal debt you can afford, base your decisions on your net income. Ratios and budgets are often calculated on gross income. In fact, lenders and mortgage companies will calculate loan repayment based on gross income. If you earn $4800 per month, would you bring that amount home? Therefore, you should never calculate your budget based on your gross income. Your gross income is the amount listed on paper such as pay stubs and income tax forms. You will never receive your gross income; so, when budgeting, you should ignore this figure. Your net income (take-home pay) is a significantly lesser amount, and it should be used when determining affordability. (Note: your non-mortgage debt should not exceed 15% of your income.)

It is best to minimize your debt – to have as little as possible. Keep in mind that there is good debt and bad debt. Although you may be struggling financially, there is a difference between struggling with a purpose as opposed to just aimlessly throwing away your money. Are you living paycheck-to-paycheck but have an emergency saving account, are contributing to your retirement, and aggressively paying your bills? If this describes you, you are doing better than 46% of Americans that are in debt but would be unable to cover a $400 emergency according to a Federal Reserve Bankrate 2015 study.

My client, Barbara does not concern herself with the total of her debt. She only looks at the amount of the monthly payment. She does not care if the balance is $200 or $5,000 as long as she can make the monthly payment. I explained to her that she will be paying on that same bill in 15, 20, or even 25 years. Her response was, "I'll always have bills." To some extent that may be true because you will always pay taxes, but credit card debt is not a necessity. Life happened (as it inevitably does) and she lost her job. The job loss caused her to lose her house eventually. Losing a job can take an emotional toll on you, I know from first-hand experience. Without an emergency fund and a debt reduction plan, foreclosure is imminent. When I lost my job, I did not have a lot of money saved, but I did not have enormous bills either.

There are two kinds of debt: good and bad. Good debt is defined as an obligation that delivers a positive return. It is an investment such as a mortgage, or student loans. The prize for paying on a mortgage is that you will eventually own your home. The reward for obtaining student loans is that you will get a degree. Many people have store credit cards, car leases, and Visa cards with high-interest rates. This is considered bad debt. Unfortunately, Barbara had accumulated a ton of bad debt. There is no benefit in bad debts, and it is an indication of financial irresponsibility. The below red flags are signs that you are headed for trouble:

- Paying too little: not making the minimum payment
- Paying too late: not paying on time resulting in late fees
- Missing payments: skipping payments
- Going over your credit limit
- Having too many accounts
- Repeatedly using savings to pay bills

The purpose of this book is to enlighten you on money management and personal finances *before* you encounter financial hardships. However, if you are experiencing any of the above conditions and you are unable to resolve the issue, please seek help immediately. There is a possibility of negotiating the amounts owed and settling old collection debts. Frequently, creditors will settle for substantially less than the amount owed. If you agree with a creditor, be sure to get the terms in writing before you submit payment. CAUTION: When a creditor settles for less than the account balance, you may owe the IRS if the forgiven amount exceeds $600. The IRS treats the forgiven debt as income which means that you would owe income taxes. Seek counsel from your tax preparer.

"Weeping may endure for a night, but joy cometh in the morning."
~ Psalm 30:5 (KJV)

Debt elimination options

If you want to reduce or eliminate your debt, you must make decisions on how to proceed with your debt reduction plan. I will show you two strategies, and you can decide which one works best. You may even decide on a combination of these options.

Avalanche option:

Card Name	Balance	Interest Rate	Minimum Payment
Visa	$2000	21%	$60
Discover	$4000	18%	$120
FavoriteStore	$800	15%	$25
Mastercard	$3500	12%	$105

The first option is the Avalanche method. This method focuses on eliminating debts with the highest interest rates and continuing to pay the bills off in descending order. In this example, you will apply your efforts toward the Visa (interest rate of 21%) while paying the minimum payments on Discover, FavoriteStore, and Mastercard. Once you have paid the Visa off, you will pay Discover $180 ($60 + $120) until it is paid off. Then, you will pay $205 ($60 + $120 + $25) on FavoriteStore until it is paid. Eventually, you will pay Mastercard $310 ($60 + $120 + $25 + $105) each month.

Snowball option:

Card Name	Balance	Interest Rate	Minimum Payment
FavoriteStore	$800	15%	$25
Visa	$2000	21%	$60
Mastercard	$3500	12%	$105
Discover	$4000	18%	$120

The second option is the Snowball method which works similar to the Avalanche method except you will concentrate on paying off the lowest balance first while paying the minimum payment on all other cards. In this example, you would pay as much as possible on the FavoriteStore card. Once you have paid off the $800, you would use that minimum payment of $25 to apply toward the Visa payment. Therefore, you would make a monthly Visa payment of $85 ($25 + $60). After the FavoriteStore card is paid off, you would apply its minimum payment of $25 and the Visa payment of $60 toward the Mastercard payment which will bring the total Mastercard payment to $190 ($25 + $60 + $105). You would continue to do this until you are debt free. The Snowball method can be a motivation booster. As you see your debts decrease, you gain the necessary courage to continue with the program. However, depending on your interest rates and balances, the Avalanche method could save you hundreds of dollars more than this method.

Which method works best? Although the Avalanche method makes more financial sense, there is not a right or wrong answer. It is a personal decision. The result is the same... you will be debt-free! I have used a combination of these methods. If the card's interest rate is not extremely low, I have paid off a card with a lower balance first. Again, the balance must be low for me to consider going this route. I feel productive when I have eliminated a bill. But, I chose my strategy carefully. It would not be financially advantageous to pay off a debt with a 4% interest rate if you have debts with higher rates. If you choose to select this option temporarily, you need to follow these steps:

- Never accelerate your payments on a 0% interest rate card if you have other debts. If you have higher interest rates cards, you should not be worried about a card that is not charging you. Caution: To avoid paying retroactive fees, be sure to pay off all 0% interest rate loans before the promotion expires.

- Once you have eliminated the cards with the lower balances, refocus your attention on the highest interest rate cards. This should give you the physiological boost that you need without paying too much money for interest.

There are also websites that can aid you in strategically reducing your debt. Powerpay.org is a website created by Utah State University Extension. It is designed to provide a personalized debt elimination plan. It is an excellent service, and it is free.

"Freedom from debt is worth more than you can earn." ~ Mark Cuban

Definition of success

The genuine way to reduce debt starts with a behavior change. You must change your definition of success. Success is not how much money that you earn, the make of your car, or the size of your house. Many people earn a six-figure salary but are stressed out because of overwhelming debt. They live in homes that they can't afford, drive cars that they can't afford, and eat expensive meals at restaurants that they can't afford. While trying to maintain this façade, many of them are struggling to avoid foreclosure. If bill collectors are blowing up your phone, your life cannot be peaceful. Your financial peace will begin when you change your lifestyle. You must stop living-large, and spending money (using credit) that doesn't exist. Your credit score and your possessions are not tied to your worth or your success because in *all* things God works for the good of those who love him, who have been called according to his purpose (Romans 8:28).

You will automatically reap the benefits of lower debt if you approach every high dollar purchase with these questions:

- Is it a *want* or a *need?* This is a critical question. Everyone has wants, and everyone should occasionally indulge in their wants.
- Can I afford it? If you have got to shuffle and "rob Peter to pay Paul," you can't afford it.
- Will it end up in the corner of your closet eventually?
- Is it a good deal? Do not forget the value of a dollar. Stay mindful of bargains and sales.

These simple questions will help to minimize your debt. Each time that you ask yourself these questions, you will become more inclined to resist impulsive decisions, and your debt will reflect your excellent choices.

"The journey of a thousand miles begins with one step."
~ Lao Tzu

Sacrificing

I have a friend with a history of money mismanagement. I was helping her with a budget because she was having trouble paying her rent and keeping current with her car payment. As we dove deep into her financial situation, I noticed that the cell phone plan for two people cost $225 per month. Astonished, I questioned the excessive cost of this plan. I know that there are plans for under $25 per person and I could not imagine why hers was so high. She stated that the fee included the cost of their iPhones.

This is an excellent example of when discipline should have been exercised. Of course, they need phones, but is the newest version necessary? Absolutely not. When money is so tight that you do not have an emergency fund, and you are on the verge of eviction, foreclosure, or repossession – an upgraded phone should not be a priority. Buy a regular ol' inexpensive cell phone until your financial situation changes. Situations like this one will only improve over time. You must prayerfully consider all options, including bankruptcy, which will remain on your credit report for ten years.

Moving forward

We have discussed your spending motivators, goals, budgets, credit cards, and other debts; now you need to make some decisions regarding your financial future. These seemingly small decisions will impact your daily life. On the following page, I have provided a list of changes that you can incorporate into your habits. Of course, every suggestion will not fit each household. Therefore, you must choose the ones that apply to your lifestyle.

Food

- Make a list of items before going grocery shopping.
- When eating at restaurants, order water instead of soda.
- Buy in bulk and separate item the items.
- Cut up your own vegetables instead of buying pre-cut veggies.
- Reduce eating out by preparing meals in advance.
- Carry leftovers for lunch.
- Freeze leftovers for a future meal.
- Buy locally made Wines (check the alcohol content to be sure it is comparable to your favorite brand).
- Buy store brand items instead of name brands.
- Use Coupons.

Household

- Unplug all appliances that are not in use, i.e., iron, can opener, etc.
- Turn heat down 1-2 degrees at night (if necessary, put on a sweater or add an extra blanket).
- Use new (spiral) energy efficient light bulbs.
- If you leave a room, turn off the lights.
- Buy a water pitcher and filter instead of bottled water.
- Reduce your television cable package, and use an alternative, such as a streaming device.
- If you have a cellphone, consider canceling your landline phone service.
- Postpone upgrading appliances until you can afford to pay cash (Will a stainless-steel refrigerator keep your food colder?)
- If you have a lawn service, reduce the service by alternating between doing

it yourself and hiring the service.
- Minimize using the Air Conditioner by using ceiling fans.
- If you usually go to bed with your tv. on, put it on sleep mode before lying down.
- Use a programmable thermostat.
- Winterize your windows and weatherize doors.
- Add attic insulation.

Personal
- If your Doctor approves, get generic prescription medicines.
- Take advantage of out-of-season items, i.e., buy summer items at the end of summer and fall items at the end of fall/winter.
- Visit thrift and consignment shops. You can find designer clothes at rock bottom prices!
- Do your own manicure and pedicure and wear closed-toe shoes in the winter.
- Stretch out your hairstyle. If you usually go to the salon weekly, go every 10-14 days.
- Travel in your home state. You would be surprised at what you are missing.
- Buy personal items (i.e., toilet paper, dish and laundry detergent) in bulk.

Finances
- Maintain a good credit score.
- Have your bills automatically drafted from your account.
- Compare interest rates. Ask if your credit card rate can be reduced or seek a lower rate credit card elsewhere.
- Have your savings automatically transferred from your checking.
- Change the due dates of your bills so that they are more aligned with your pay periods.

- If your mortgage is 2% more than the prevailing rates, consider refinancing.
- Defer your student loans (only in dire circumstances).
- Buy a reliable car (Google: Cars that get 200k miles).
- Carpool or use public transportation.
- Trade your expensive car for one that is more affordable.
- Unless your car specifically requires premium gas, use regular or mid-grade gas.
- Consult with your insurance agent about dropping collision and/or comprehensive insurance on vehicles over ten years old.
- Downgrade your apartment/house for a more affordable home.
- Get your home and auto insurance with the same company.
- Increase insurance deductibles (it lowers the premium).
- Buy term insurance (it is less expensive than Whole Life).
- Only use ATMs in your bank's network.
- When possible, pay cash for purchases.
- Get a lower cell phone plan.
- If your company offers matching retirement funds such as a 401k plan, enroll as soon as possible. It is free money!
- Thoroughly read your company's benefits package and sign up for all applicable benefits.
- Get a 2nd job. Find a way to earn some extra cash.

Implementing some of the suggestions will be seamless while others will be a little harder. Keep in mind that to progress, you must shift your priorities. It is a part of a mature financial plan. Also, you must think outside of the box. Jackie, a single, divorced mother, has four kids. She uses a list when going grocery shopping. But, she took it a bit further. She plans her family's meals for each day of the week and drafts her shopping list according to the ingredients for each meal. For example, if she were planning a spaghetti dinner, her shopping list would look like this:

- noodles
- sauce
- cheese
- ground turkey/beef
- onion
- garlic bread
- eggs
- lettuce
- tomato
- salad dressing

Jackie drastically reduced her grocery bill by only buying food that was necessary to prepare the weekly meals.

Again, every suggestion will not work for everybody, but do what works best for you.

> "Don't judge each day by the harvest you reap, but by the seeds that you plant." ~ Robert Louis Stevenson

Notes

RoslynLash.com

Reflections

I want to share a quote by Gordon Hinckley~ "You will come to know that what appears today to be a sacrifice will prove instead to be the greatest investment that you will ever make." As a young adult, I saved a little, and although it was a small amount, those minor financial sacrifices lead to my most significant investments. They have allowed me to be semi-retired, and to feed myself after my job loss. If I had not somewhat prepared for the unexpected, I would not have the luxury of writing this book. I want to educate as many people as possible so that they can adequately prepare for their future. A wise person can learn from the experiences of others. I hope that you have learned from my experiences as well as from the lessons shared in this book.

And now, I am going to request something from you. If you have found any of this information helpful, please leave an Amazon review. Just go to Amazon.com and type *The 7 Fruits Of Budgeting* in the search box. Click on the reviews and click *write a review*. As I proceed on my journey as an Author, your review will help me to evolve. Lastly, I'd like to share my hopes for your future. I hope that you will give a little more than you expect and receive much more than you dream. May God continue to bless you in all your endeavors!

"May your choices reflect your hopes, not your fears."
~ Nelson Mandela

Oh, that God would bless you indeed,
and enlarge your territory.
I pray that his hand will be with you,
and that he will keep you from evil,
so that you may not cause pain.
~ Based on the Prayer of Jabez
(1 Chronicles 4:10 NKJV)

Acknowledgments

I would like to thank Emma Trotman for reading the entire book and providing her excellent feedback. I also owe a debt of gratitude to my cousin, Faith Davis, and my friends, Delores Butler, Turquoise Corbett, and Donna Settle. As my focus group, you provided me with valuable suggestions and encouragement. I love and appreciate each of you.

About the Author

Roslyn Lash, the Ol' Skool Money Mentor, is a Financial Educator, Coach, Speaker, and now an Author. She is passionate about helping millennials navigate through their finances so that they can live more purposefully. She is a Real Estate Broker and is also the Founder of Youth Smart Financial Education Services which specializes in financial literacy.

Roslyn has always been good at managing her money. Her abilities became publicly known after she happily survived a job loss and became an Accredited Financial Counselor. Her advice has been featured in *Huffington Post, Los Angeles Times, NASDAQ, TIME, USA Today*, and a host of other media outlets.

The strategies in this book, *The 7 Fruits of Budgeting*, have allowed her to do more of what she enjoys and to live a more fruitful life. Her tips are simple, easy to understand, and easy to implement so that you too can live fruitfully! You can follow her on social media:

- Facebook Community: Smart Savers Supreme group
- Facebook: Roslyn Lash
- Twitter: @RosLash
- Website: RoslynLash.com

Appendix

All Forms are available for download at RoslynLash.com

Card Name	Balance	Interest Rate	Minimum Payment	Account Number
Totals	$			

Regular Budget

Home	Cost
Rent/Mortgage	
Property Taxes	
Insurance	
Homeowner's Dues	
Utilities	
Home phone	
Cell phone	
Home repairs/maintenance	
Yard	
Security Alarm	
Other:	

Other:	
Daily Expenses	**Cost**
Food	
Child care	
Animal food/care	
Other:	
Other:	
Transportation	**Cost**
Car Payment	
Gas	
Insurance	
Repairs	
Parking	

Public Transportation	
Car tags & title & inspection	
Property taxes	
Other:	
Other:	

Entertainment	Cost
Restaurants	
Movies/Plays	
Concerts	
Subscriptions or Fees	
Other:	
Other:	

Health	Cost
Health club dues	
Insurance	
Prescriptions	
Over the counter meds	
Co-Payments	
Life Insurance	
Other:	
Other:	
Other:	
Vacation	**Cost**
Transportation	
Accommodations	

Food	
Activities	
Pet Boarding	
Souvenirs	
Other:	
Other:	
Dues	**Cost**
Charity	
Magazines	
Religious Organizations	
Other:	
Other:	

Personal	Cost
Clothes	
Toiletries	
Hair	
Salon/Spa	
Other:	
Other:	
Financial	**Cost**
Emergency Savings	
Long-term savings	
Retirement	
Credit Card #1	
Credit Card #2	

Credit Card #3	
Credit Card #4	
Loan #1:	
Loan #2:	
Other:	
Other:	
	Total Cost: $

Variable Budget:

Variable Expense	Cost
	Variable Total Cost: $

Notes

www.ingramcontent.com/pod-product-compliance
Lightning Source LLC
Chambersburg PA
CBHW082340220526
45470CB00008B/2575